Ramadan Poems Written by Homeschooled Children

The Confident Ummah

Copyright © 2023

All rights reserved. Without limiting rights under the copyright reserved above, no part of this publication may be reproduced, stored, introduced into a retrieval system, distributed or transmitted in any form or by any means, including without limitation photocopying, recording, or other electronic or mechanical methods, without the prior written permission of the publisher, except in the case of brief quotations embodied in critical reviews and certain other non-commercial uses permitted by copyright law.

The scanning, uploading, and/or distribution of this document via the internet or via any other means without the permission of the publisher is illegal and is punishable by law. Please purchase only authorized editions and do not participate in or encourage electronic piracy of copyrightable materials

About The Book

As we know, Ramadan is a sacred month for Muslims. We fast from sunrise to sunset and spend the day performing as many good deeds, voluntary prayers and Qur'an reading as possible. The evenings are busy with breaking our fasts and rushing back to the mosques in order to pray some more.

We then end this special month with a joyful celebration called Eid al-Fitr.

This book of poems is a compilation of poems that were composed during the month of Ramadan, by our local community of homeschooled children - with a touch of help from their parents. The poems offer a wonderful insight into each child's individual experience and feelings during this blessed month.

We hope to take you on a spiritual journey through our poetry collection.

Enjoy!

Back cover illustrators: Sahara-Amel aged 9, Haroon Axworthy aged 8, Musa Axworthy aged 6, Aaishah Ali aged 9, Nusaibah Siddique, Sarah Tony Ahmad and Yusuf Qureshi aged 10.

Contents

The Way to Have Fun, by Musa Qureshi	5
Acrostic Poem on Ramadan, by Ammina Master	6
The Blessed Month, by Iman Irfan	7
Ramadan is Here, by Sahara - Amel	8
Ramadan like a Flower by Madeeha & Hameeda Alam	9
The Sleepless Night, by Musa Fawzi	10
A Special Month, by Fatimah Sultan	11
Acrostic Poem on Ramadan, by Aminah	12
Will the Skies..., by Azmena Ali	13
The Beauty of Ramadan, by Zubayr Alam	14
The Month of the Qur'an, by Ruqayyah Ditta	15
Glory to..., by Ali	16
Rearing to go Jannah, by Maddie, Mimi & Zuby	17
Ramadan, the Best Month, by Ammar Jakhura	18
Ramadan has Come, by Alia Jakhura	19
I love Ramadan, by Ameera Jakhura	20
Inner reflections	21

My First Fast, by Faisal Iqkhawaja	22
Staying up for Iftar, by Haroon Axworthy	23
I Love Ramadan, by Musa Axworthy	24
My Love for the All-Mighty	25
Laylatul Qadr, by Sameeha Mehreen	26
The Holy Month of the Qur'an, by Aishah Ali	27
Assalamu alaikum Ramadan	28
Ramadan Acrostic Poem, by Yusuf Qureshi	29
Al-Malik, Ar-Rahman	30
I Shed a Tear, by Sumaiyah Shannon	31
What?! No Samosas! By Eesa Shannon	32
O Ramadan, by Aisha Nadat	33
Iqra Iqra Iqra, by Muhammad Sufiyan	35
Treasures of Ramadan, by Muhammad	37
Solace in the Ramadan Moon	38
Ramadan is Here, by Sarah Tony Abraham	39
Iftar Time, by Yahya Yousha Hussain	40
Ramadan Poem, by Nusaibah Z Siddique	41
The End of Ramadan	42

Musa's Ramadan
The way to have fun!

Ramadan is soon, when we see the moon.

It's only noon and I'm looking for my spoon.

It's the month of June, Eid is soon.

We made some tune's and popped balloon's.

It's Ramadan, it's time to have fun.

Pray Salah and remember Allah (SWT).

It's Ramadan, we read Quran.

By Musa Qureshi

Age 6

Acrostic Poem on Ramadan

Rushing to the masjid to Jannah.

A beautiful masjid shines with light.

Month of mercy, month of the Qur'an.

Adthan and Qur'an in a beautiful way.

Duas - May Allah accept them all.

A month of forgiveness, a month of love.

New Moon signals the beginning and the end, we love you Ramadan.

By Aamina Master
Age 8

The Blessed Month

Knock knock
Someone is at the door. Who could it be?
I wonder as I go and see
I open the door and see this is no stranger to me and my family

Ramadan Ramadan!!!
The month of the Quran, the month
when the big devils are tied up and the doors of hell are locked, and the doors of Heaven are wide open
Your good deeds multiply and your bad deeds are forgiven

We fast for Allah from dawn to dusk
It may seem hard, but it is a really easy task
With all that yummy food, we look forward to when we open our fast
Throughout the month, we weep and repent for all the bad deeds that we did in the past

Allah(swt) is al-Ghaffar the most forgiving
Allah(swt) is so merciful
That If you give charity,
Allah(swt) will give you shade on the day of judgement

Let's not forget Laylatul-Qadr the 10 blessed nights
So do more good deeds and you will be full of glee
A feeling of sadness fills the heart that Ramadan will soon depart, so let's do as much as we can for it is still Ramadan and may Allah forgive all our bad deeds
Ameen   **By Iman Irfan**

Ramadan is here!

Ramadan is here, I can't wait to fast , then in one month is Eid will come , "Oh please come fast "!

I hear the adhaan, it's time to pray then I can go and play.

I'm going to give some dates, let me get the plates.
We start with the dates, next is chicken and rice , with juicy strawberries for after. "Oh how nice"!

It's maybe the last day of Ramadan and now we need to go and catch a sight of the moon.
Hurrah I can't believe it will be Eid soon.

I'm so happy Eid is here , although I can't wait for Ramadan again next year.

By Sahara - Amel

Ramadan like a Flower

Ramadan is like a flower that blooms once a year,

Ramadan, a flower that leaves a lingering scent of musk which emanate from fasting mouths inhaled by angels,

Ramadan, a descending flower that breathes the spring of life, our Quran

Ramadan, a flower that contains honey so sweet that it makes eyes drool for it's taste,

Ramadan, a flower that spreads its beauty to hearts that bloom with it,

Ramadan, a flower that's moonlit so it, spread it's light to faces that shine with it,

Ramadan, a flower so soft that it melts the hardest of hearts,

Ramadan, a flower so rare that we only see it once a year,

Ramadan, a flower given to all for free with a night of power,

I love my Ramadan flower

**By Twins Madeeha and Hameeda Alam,
Age 8 with mum**

The Sleepless Night

The day is about to begin

It is time to dig in

For yet the unsleepable night has past

And the fun will last and last

Ramadan has past

Yet Eid is about to begin

By Musa Fawzi
Age 10

A Special Month

Ramadan is a special month for us Muslims.

And it brings lots of blessings from Allah.

More and more rewards we get.

And we offer more Ibadah in this Holy Month.

Duas are accepted by Allah.

And different and delicious foods are made for iftar.

Not only do people fast, they take care of the poor and needy for extra reward in the month of Ramadan.

By Fatimah Sultan
Age 7

Acrostic Poem on Ramadan

Remembering

Allah

Morning

Afternoon

Day

And

Night

By Aminah
Age 4

Will the Skies...

Will the skies mourn too for the Ramadan moon?
What will she witness in its absence for it shall leave us soon,
Will the skies look down and shed some tears,
When heedlessness again begins to appear?
Will they grumble and moan in thunder and pain, for the evil that returns once again?
The skies that looked down and saw pleading palms raised upturned,
Released their angels and anticipated a warm return,
I wonder if the skies clutch the thinning crescent so tight,
knowing for Allah it will leave our sight,
For divine words that ascend from musky mouths will adjourn,
And dwindle away with the moon's bittersweet sojourn,
prostrating hearts will mourn for the springtime bloom,
That wither away with the Ramadan moon,
Breaking skies and hearts torn asunder,
Will they be united with grief for Ramadan I wonder?

By Azmena Ali

The Beauty of Ramadan

A long time ago on a special night in Ramadan,
The Quran came down and landed upon,
A sacred tablet in the lowest sky,
To where our past and future deeds are stored up high,
My mum says in Surah al Qadr it has been said,
That all these deeds by Allah has been set,
One powerful night angels come to earth to carry out the year's decrees,
And so millions of Muslims love to worship that night instead of sleep,
And if we worship Allah that special night in Ramadan,
We get rewards worth a 1000 nights of worship like we've actually done,
And all our past sins can even be erased,
All because to Allah we have prayed,
In Ramadan we change habits and give up even normal things,
Like eating and drinking in the day, to help as keep away from smaller sins,
There's lots of wisdom why we have Ramadan,
I'm so grateful that to us it has been blessed upon

By Zubayr Alam
Age 9

The Month of the Qur'an

Ramadan is the month of the Quran
And there is an extra prayer
Mercy is all around in this month
And you should not fight
Dawn till dusk you must not eat
Angel's come down with their light
Now it's time to celebrate Eid.

By Ruqayyah Ditta
Age 8

Glory To...

Glory to His pen that wrote down all our fate,

Glory to His Greatness that honours us by His Grace,

Glory to The house of honour that preserves The Sacred Tablet,

Glory to this night that angels descend with decrees to establish,

Glory to the angels our guests so eager to meet us,

Glory to the heavenly scriptures that to all hearts He reaches,

Glory to this night of sweet serenity, peace until the breaking of the dawn,

Glory to this month of mercy which we seek to train our body, hearts and souls to call Him when we fall,

Glory to The month of patience which we learn self-restraint,

Glory to this month where remembrances of His highness we train to eternally fixate

By Ali

Rearing to go to Jannah

Rearing to go to Jannah

Away from anxiety to peace in Ramadan

Medicine for the heart is the Quran

Allah more than all doctors loves to help

Discombobulated patients never fear

Allahs beautiful words are so clear

Nobody heals like Allah does

By Maddie, Mimi and Zuby

Ramadan, the Best Month

Ramadan, Ramadan – the best month of the year.
This is the month we must all fast
From suhoor at dawn until iftaar at sunset.

In Ramadan all Muslims do lots of good deeds.
We pray, read Quran, give charity and make lots of dua.
The rewards are 70 times more!

In the last ten days of Ramadan,
There is a night called Laylatul-Qadr.
This is the night we worship Allah
Throughout the night.

On that night we must say the dua
that Aisha ra said.
And we are promised by Allah,
That all our past sins will be forgiven.

Laylatul-Qadr is very special.
It is when the Quran was revealed.
Doing charity during this month is very special too.
Because we remember those who are in need,
Those who live in war, those who are ill and those who are just less
fortunate.

We must also remember,
Those who fast will enter Jannah,
through a special gate called ar-Rayan.
In this month we must do all that will please Allah.

By Ammar Jakhura

Ramadan has come!

Ramadan has come. It comes every year.
All the Muslims wait for it to come.
We stare at the sky in the evening,
And look for a crescent moon.
We say the dua and start fasting.
We don't eat or drink from dawn to sunset.
We also try to be more kind.
When someone fights we must say 'I'm fasting, I'm fasting'.

In Ramadan we get 70 rewards for one good deed.
To earn these rewards you should help your mum.
You could help her clean or cook iftar.
This is the month we think about
Our Muslim sisters and brothers a lot.
We give charity and donations,
To help those who are in need.

We like to give eid gifs,
To the poor children who don't get a lot.
We also get lots of gifts,
From our family and friends.

But don't forget,
We must read Quran and make duas.
It is when we get the best chance
For our duas to come true.
Duas are certainly answered
When made before breaking the fast.

In the last 10 days there is Laylatul Qadr
And the dua we must learn and say at that night is
Allohumma innaka afuwwun, tuhibbul 'afwa, fa'fu anni
Oh Allah, you are most forgiving, you love to forgive, so forgive me.
How special Ramadan is !

By Alia Jakhura

I Love Ramadan

O Allah, we will fast in Ramadan
We will make wudu, pray and read Quran.
We will also make lots of dua

We Listen to Allah and do as he says.
We must also listen to our mummies and daddies too.
We help washing dishes, making food and baking.

Thank you Allah for giving us food and toys.
Thank you Allah for our parents and grandparents.
I love you Allah and will always do!

By Ameera Jakhura

Inner Reflections

We all have dark speckles of sins,

Many deeply embedded deep within,

My dear there is no weakness in admitting your weakness,

There is no shame in exposing your softness,

Guided is the one who knows this and opens herself to The One who gives her shade, water and sun,

Sacred sunlight of guidance absolve the sins,

So we may never burn due to the mercy of Ramadan blessings.

My First Fast

I am a 7 years old boy and it's my first time to fast.
I know Ramadan has begun because a new moon has now passed.
Ramadan is the month of forgiveness, 'may my sins be burnt away', I asked.

On my first day of fasting I felt new to it.
I felt hungry and thirsty but I knew I wouldn't quit!
I felt extra hungry when my younger siblings were given sweet, juicy fruits, I admit.
I would leave the room and start reading Qur'an because it will help me submit.

Because it was my fist time, I would spend time thinking about my Iftar.
But my mummy and Abu would help me by giving me activities to do to keep me busy because Iftar was so far.
I would play pictionary. I like playing naughts and crosses too.
My stomach is so empty, I never need the loo!

It's Iftar time! I start off with water, almonds and dates.
Then I slowly make my way over, my cooked food awaits.
I don't feel hungry anymore, Hurrah!
I say my Dua's and finish off with Alhamdullilah!
Than I go to pray Maghrib but I'm too tired to pray Taraweeh Salah.
Mabye I can go when I am bigger, about 9 or 10, Insha'Allah.

I end the day, I am feeling so proud.
'I knew I could do it', I say out loud.

I hope my fasts are accepted because I tried my best!
I managed to fast the whole day, even I am impressed!

By Faisal Iqkhawaja & Mum
Age 7

Staying up for Iftaar

On the 15th of Ramadan I stayed up for iftaar.
It was exciting.
We did it on the 6th night as well.

First I started to tidy up in the room, then I got some food out of the fridge.
We had kebab pastries (patis) that Maa made.
I put a date on everyone's plate.
I put the chickpeas on the table.
We sat and said the du'a, 'Allahumma....' and broke our fast. I had missed dinner and when I broke my fast it felt amazing.
Even if it wasn't my favourite food it would have tasted good I'm sure.

The patis tasted amazing with mayonnaise and ketchup.
We ate some food that our neighbour gave for iftaar, it was so yummy.
We gave our neighbours some biscuits that I baked on their plate.

Maa and Abbu prayed maghrib while I finished my iftaar and I enjoyed the baklava that Nana and Nanu gave.
It was so fun staying up for iftaar.
Maybe next year I will stay up for more inshaAllah and I will go for taraweeh in the masjid more than once.

By Haroon Axworthy
Age 8

I love Ramadan

I can do more good deeds because I get more reward for them.
It's the month the Qur'an came down.
Laylatul Qadr is inside it.

Sometimes I stay up for iftaar.
Yummy foods like dates, kebab pastries and haleem.
We put up decorations.
I have a calendar that I get to take a good deed card and a question card out – and sometimes a chocolate!

I get to give money to the poor.
I try to fast to get good deeds, if it was difficult Allah wouldn't ask us to do it.
There's a gate in Jannah that people who fast go through.

We get to read Ramadan stories.
We get to watch taraweeh on the computer.
We get to listen to Names of Allah with The Azharis.
We give our neighbours dates so they eat them and their fast counts for us.
Our neighbours give us some food too.
We make chocolate chip biscuits and flapjacks and share them.

By Musa Axworthy
Age 6

My Love for the All-Mighty

You feel hunger, oh yes gut-wrenched,

The loss of water made you appreciate the quench,

Took the loss of food to appreciate the satiation,

Heedful hearts turning hands up in supplication,

Fasting, turning hearts in gratitude,

God turning hearts with much love for you,

Blessings we take granted of deserves more praise,

Thank again because He rewards with more, your ranks then raised,

Thanks after thanks, reward after reward, blessings after blessings,

To be grateful in itself requires abilities which deserve more thanks professing

Laylatul Qadr

Laylatul Qadr, a night so full of power

When Allah's mercy is like a shower

In the breeze the trees will bow

And day by day your imaan will grow

Its somewhere in the last ten night

So search and search with all your might

In the breeze the grass shall sway

So for this night don't look away

And make Dua, for it could be granted

Raise your hands and keep them slanted

By Sameeha Mehreen.

The Holy Month of the Qur'an

The holy month of the Quran, Ramadan, is a special time to pray,
Our Lord is Allah and Him, let's not disobey.
We were over the moon when it started,
But devastated when it departed.
Shaytan, the accursed, was locked up,
From dawn to dusk, not even water did we sup.

If we become angry,
We won't have much glory.
Fasting,
Its effects are lasting.
We cry tears of sadness when Ramadan is gone,
The month in which we didn't even have an ice-cream cone.

O Allah, O Allah, please guide me,
I don't want my sins to sting me like a bee.
O Allah, O Allah, please forgive me,
For your sake, I won't even drink tea.
You are the One,
Who can forgive every one,
So please forgive us our Lord,
And instead of mischief, we will play board games when we are bored.

Oh Ramadan, Ramadan – a time for mercy,
A month in which our souls are kept busy,
We remember Allah in the day and into the night,
Give up bad deeds – even if we want to fight.

Our special guest, a month sent to make us better,
In which our beloved prophet received, of the Quran, the first letter.
As we bid you farewell,
We pray we meet again with many more tales of goodness to tell.

By Aaishah Ali
Age 9

Assalamu alaikum Ramadan

You are the month of mercy when shaytan is locked up, the month of goodness.
All over the world people look forward to your visit.
We count down the days and search the skies for the crescent moon.
For the sake of Allah Muslims fast, they skip lunch and only eat dinner.
Before Fajr time kids and adults wake up for suhoor, the early morning meal,
Because our noble prophet told us there is blessing in it.

When the adhan starts everyone stops eating and their fast begins.
All over the world we hear, "Allahu Akbar, Allahu Akbar,"
And the muaddhin reminds us that, "assalatu khairu-min-an-nawm",
Prayer is better than sleep.
When you are with us our days and nights are extra special.

At the end of the day families sit together waiting patiently.
When Muslims hear the call of maghrib prayer they break their fasts with the words,
"The thirst has gone, the veins have been moistened and the reward is there, insha'Allah.
They break their fast with a nutritious date, drink some water and go to the mosque to pray.
When they return home they eat the delicious food prepared for them.

We have special memories of being allowed to stay up a little later and pray taraweeh and visit the mosque.
We really enjoy your visit and miss you so much when you leave.
We hope that we are able to remember the lessons you have taught us and become better Muslims,
Until the next time we meet insha'Allah.

By Abdur-Raheem Ali
Age 7

Ramadan Acrostic Poem

Ramadan is our guest.

After Suhoor you've got to fast.

Muhammad (saw) brought the Quran.

Angel Jibrail gave the Prophet the Quran.

Dua is always accepted in noble Ramadan.

Always be kind not grumpy when fasting!

Now is the time to memorise the Quran.

By Yusuf Qureshi
Age 9

Al-Malik, Ar-Rahman

He's opened the gates of paradise for you,
The abode above is adorned for you,
His generosity is calling to you,
He invites you to be His special guests and friends,
To be greeted with such and love care,
How could you not yearn to be with Him there?

Just the knowledge of these heaven's doors,
Whispers peace into your heart,
Just the knowledge of these guarded doors,
Yields you to want to explore heavenly art,
Wouldn't you want to be greeted by angels with whom He hosts?
Wouldn't you want to be swept through doors of gardens that He owns?

I Shed a Tear

There is always one special time of the year,
When I think about it, I shed a tear.

It's the blessed month of Ramadhan,
The month of the noble Qur'an.

We have the opportunity to strengthen our eemaan,
And also to strengthen making du'a.

I think about how blessed we are,
To be alive this Ramadhan.

I hope you understand why I shed a tear,
Maybe I'll shed another tear next year.

By Sumaiyah Shannon

What?! No Samosas!

The house has gone mad!
But I'm terribly sad.
Because in my house there is not a single samosa!
Not even a pakora!
It's Ramadhaan tonight,
Because the moon is in sight.
The world's gone ecstatic.
And everyone's getting stuff from their attic.
The gates of Jannah are flung open,
Every Ramadhaan this happens.
And the gates of Jahannam are slammed shut.
So, the devil is locked up.

Now it's the tenth day of Ramadhaan,
But for dinner we've only had chicken and naan!
I'm not in a good mood.
Because I'm sick of this food!
"I'm just popping into the shop for some samosas,
And the ingredients for some pakoras!"

By Eesa Shannon
Age 8

O Ramadan

As we wait for the arrival of the blessed beautiful month,
with all its glory and splendour it brings.
The doors of heaven have opened.....
We feel a sense of relief, consolation and comfort.....
Like waiting for a child you haven't seen for 11 months, or
Like a fierce longing for something you really need, or,
Like a child waiting and yearning for the comfort of their
mother.....

O Ramadan, a salvation for the 11 months, where we were
lost in feeding our physical desires,
And ignoring our spiritual.

O Ramadan....
The ruh is starved, neglected.....
You are a saviour for our souls,
A chance to press the pause button, and reflect, contemplate
make amends....

O, those beautiful nights, where we are in deep whisper
with our creator, most High.
Where we pour out our hearts,
Complain of our weaknesses,
We promise ' Never ever again.....'
In the hope of pardon, to the most Merciful.

O for those night prayers....
The ambience in the masjid,
The tilawat echoing within the walls,
The love and unity sensed by all,
The dhikr and duas....

O blessed Ramadan, you are truly the loved one.....
A reminder of what we should be and what we can.
A chance at a reflection of our sinful lives,
A chance to make a plea for our mistakes,
To reconnect and mend ties with the One.

O Ramadan....
Slow down....
You come and go like a blink of an eye,
A reminder that our lives will do the same.
O Ramadan.....
Slow down.....
We have not yet had our fill of you.
Truly ' A limited number of days' as Allah described you.

O Ramadan.....

By Aisha Nadat.

Iqra Iqra Iqra

Iqra Iqra Iqra
Iqra bismi rab bikal lazee khalaq
Khalaqal insaana min 'Alaq
Iqra wa Rab bukal Akram
Al lazee 'allama bil qalam

Read Read Read
Read The Noble Quran
Read in the name of your LORD
The one who created you
Read in the name of your lord
The one who is most generous to you
Read in the name of your lord
Who Taught by the pen to you
Read In the name of your lord
That which was Unknown to you
Read Read Read
Read The Noble Quran
Read in the name of your lord
The book revealed to the mankind

Read in the name of your lord
To stay rewarded and be kind
Read in the name of your lord
Blessed in the month of Ramadan
Read in the name of your lord
Which is the intercessor in the day of resurrection

Read Read Read
Read The Noble Quran
Read in the name of your lord
In it is the clear proof of guidance
Read the noble Quran
To attain fruitful sustenance
Read the Noble Quran
Sent to the last Prophet
Alhamdullillah which is very perfect
Read in the name of your lord
As It is a form of Ibadah
Read in the name of your lord
For every letter in it has hasanah
Read Read Read
Read the noble Quran.

By Muhammad Sufiyan

Treasures of Ramadan

Here comes the cresent moon as a sign of Ramadan,
To mark the end of shaban
With the blessings of Ar -Rahman.
Waking up for Suhoor to start your day with Dates,
Waiting untill the sunset to break your
fast with different Tastes.
Every Muslim knows his righteous deed of Fasting,
You cannot escape from the prayers and Quran Reciting.
This is the month in which Quran was
revealed to Prophet Muhammad,
Brought by Angel Jibreel to symbolize
the meaning of Tawheed.
Let's observe one of the five pillars of
Islam to boost your Emaan,
The month in which heavens are open and
chains for the Shaytan.
Waiting for the Angels during last ten
Days of Laylat Ul Qadr,
Followed with prayers of Qiyam Ul Layl .
Let's Observe the night that is better than 1000 months,
Seek the Mercy of Allah along with Forgiveness.
Here comes the crescent moon to mark
the celebration of Eid,
You cannot escape from fitra and gatherings of Masjid.

By Muhammad Sufiyan

Solace in the Ramadan Moon

Raise your gaze, come roam the skies,
Underneath The divine paradise,
Decorations of rainbow ribbons, misty fog flows,
Hearts can't help but beat poetry and prose,
Between the earth and whats kept high,
Nature wraps a hidden surprise,
With cotton candy clouds, glittery star studded canopy,
Secret gifts to which my drumming heart hums back in harmony,
With a golden brooch -a blazing bronze sun,
Hopes race high, brazenly beyond,
We'll transcend these embellishments, wrappings and layers,
With our hands held high in peaceful prayers,
Towards a piercing pearly luminous moon,
With a forthright faith we adorn ourselves too,
To see the delights of the unseen soon,
We find sweet solace in the Ramadan moon.

Ramadan is Here!

It's Ramadan, it's Ramadan, it's Ramadan

We fast in the daylight and break our fast at sunset.

Then we do it all over again.

Sarah Tony Abraham
Age 8

Iftar Time

Mat laid
Lantern lit
Sticky dates
Juicy fruits
Sweet melon
Hot kichuri
Glasses poured
Hands raised
Silent whispers
Thirst gone
Veins moistened
Reward confirmed
In shaa Allah!

**By Yahya Yousha Hussain
with a bit of help from Ammu
Age 7**

Ramadan Poem

Ramadan is here, Ramadan is here!
We prepare delicious Suhoor,
for energy throughout the day.

Ramadan is here, Ramdan is here!
It's time to break our fast.
It is time to eat iftar!
Ramadan is ending
Ramadan is gone!
Now Eid is here,
It's time for fun!

By Nusaibah Z Siddique

The End of Ramadan

Ramadan is a month of Quran, with which our hearts are over-flowing,

And if you are sad that Ramadan is going,

Then know that your Quran will never leave you,

It will travel with you to your grave soon,

The question is how do you choose to befriend your traveling partner?

Will you allow it to guide you further and farther?

Will you take your companion's advice?

To let your hand be held to paradise

www.ingramcontent.com/pod-product-compliance
Lightning Source LLC
Chambersburg PA
CBHW030459010526
44118CB00011B/1011